ANGELA
THE
ANGEL

JERAMY COLLINS

AuthorHouse™
1663 Liberty Drive
Bloomington, IN 47403
www.authorhouse.com
Phone: 833-262-8899

Because of the dynamic nature of the Internet, any web addresses or links contained in this book may have changed since publication and may no longer be valid. The views expressed in this work are solely those of the author and do not necessarily reflect the views of the publisher, and the publisher hereby disclaims any responsibility for them.

This book is printed on acid-free paper.

ISBN: 979-8-8230-3986-4 (sc)
ISBN: 979-8-8230-3988-8 (hc)
ISBN: 979-8-8230-3987-1 (e)

Library of Congress Control Number: 2024926116

Print information available on the last page.

Published by AuthorHouse   12/12/2024

authorHOUSE®

Angela the Angel

Jeramy Collins

Hello there, my friends.
Gather 'round, find a seat.
I am Angela the Angel. I'm
so glad we could meet.
I am here to help answer your
questions about Heaven.
No matter if you are two
or one hundred eleven.

My small size might fool you, but I'm a true angel pro.
I am a super helper angel, just so you know.
While I was in angel school, I was third in my class.

But there were only three angels,
so I was technically last.

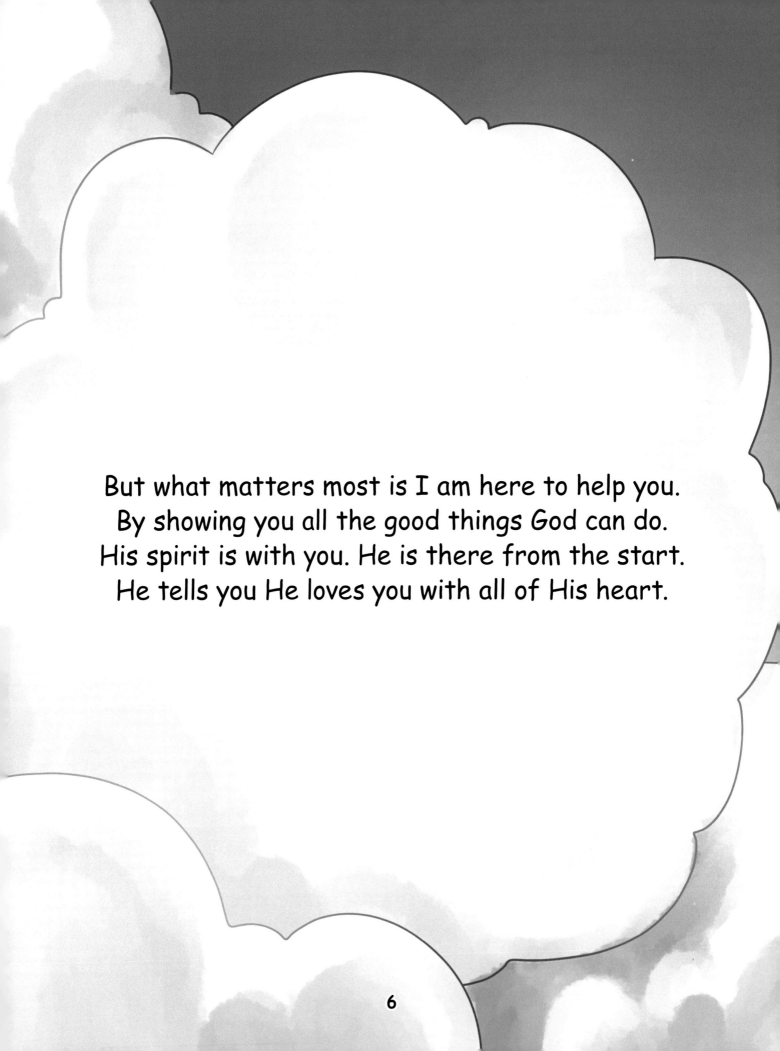

But what matters most is I am here to help you.
By showing you all the good things God can do.
His spirit is with you. He is there from the start.
He tells you He loves you with all of His heart.

But if God is speaking, does He shout? Does He sing? You listen all day, but do not hear a thing.

8

He is speaking to
you, friends. Trust
me. Believe.
I can teach you
how He does it,
with some tricks
up my sleeve.

I wave my arms 'round,
and you'll hear a loud

BOOM.

And the next thing you know,
we are out of this room.
And now here we are at ...

A cave near a mountain?
Oh no! I'm so sorry. Now
how did this happen?

14

But wait, over there, coming out of the cave.
There sits an old man who is looking quite grave.
It's alright my friends. There is no need to fear.
His name is Elijah. Let's get closer and hear.

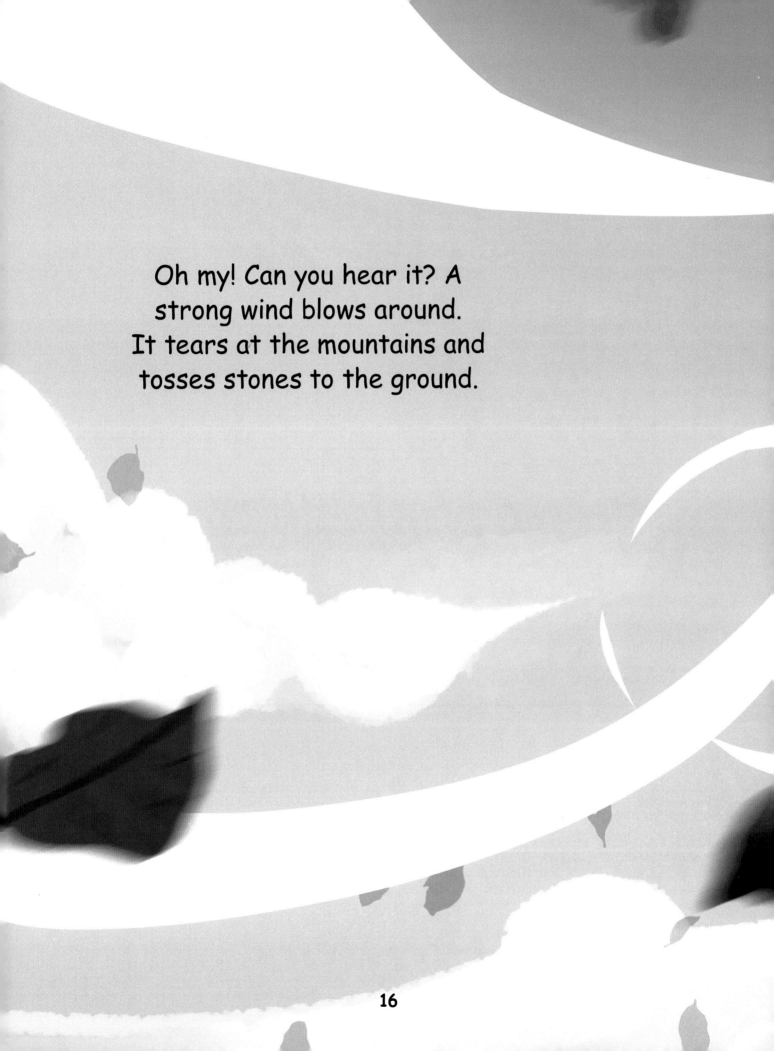

Oh my! Can you hear it? A strong wind blows around. It tears at the mountains and tosses stones to the ground.

You can't hear a thing
but the wind in the air.
But through all this noise,
God still is not there.

The wind dies down, and the earth begins breaking.
I'm stumbling and tumbling from all of the shaking.
But nothing is speaking from the rumbling ground.
Because, my dear friends, God's voice is not found.

And right after that comes a fiery light.
The heat is intense as it fills up the night.
This fire is strong, and I'm starting to sweat.
But just like before, God isn't here yet.

All of the noise makes it hard, I admit it.
But listen in the quiet. If you try, you can hear it.
It is not in a fire, an earthquake, or twister.
It's in a still, small voice. No more than a whisper.

Now the Prophet Elijah
wraps his cloak on his face.
And hearing God's voice
made this a special place.
Elijah knew how to block
out all the noise.
And hear what he knew
was God's true voice.

You see boys and girls,
God's not a mystery.
He has always been the same
through all of history.
He can scream using earthquakes
and even through fire.
But sharing His love is
what He truly desires.

Be like our friend, Elijah, and
you'll never go wrong.
You can all learn to hear God.
It doesn't take long.

If you pray in the quiet, and
you pull out your Bible.
You'll learn to know His voice
in just a short while.

Sometimes it seems boring with no toys and no stuff.
But when you hear God speak, He is more than enough.
So let's all hear God's voice. That is my prayer for you.
God loves you so much, and I love you too.

Printed in the United States
by Baker & Taylor Publisher Services